Project 120

Project
120

Hearing God's Voice and Following Him

Anne M. Cochran

Anne M. Cochran

GGP

Glory Girl Publishing

GGP

Glory Girl Publishing

P.O. Box 11297
Charlotte, NC 28220

www.GloryGirlPublishing.com

Anne@GloryGirlPublishing.com

Cover and interior text design by
Brett James Miller
www.bjm-bookdesign.com

Cover image: © Fotolia/oksix

ISBN: 978-0-9909865-6-0

Editorial Note: Scripture references are from
-King James Version
-New International Version
-New Living Translation

For Hallie and Rob

"No eye has seen, no ear has heard, no mind has imagined what God has prepared for those how love him. But it was to us that God revealed these things by his Spirit. For his Spirit searches out everything and shows us God's deep secrets."

—1 Corinthians 2:9-10

Contents

Project 120

Acknowledgments

This book would not have come to be if the Holy Spirit had not spoken a word to me one morning in December 2013. I am so thankful that I know Him and that I am able to hear His Voice. Holy Spirit, thank You for being my friend.

Betsy Thorpe, thank you again for helping me make this project come to life. Your input, your wisdom, and your gifting made my dream of publishing a second book a reality. I love working with you! Maybe we will get to do it again!

Thanks to Maya Packard, the copyeditor, and to Brett Miller, the book designer. The finishing touches make this little book special and unique.

To Allen Faubion, who agreed to write a blurb for the back cover. Your ministry, your mentoring, and your willingness to come alongside me means more than you can know. To you and my GOZ family, thank you for your love and support.

And to Rob, my husband, who financed this book. You have always unconditionally loved and supported me in my walk with the

Lord and in my hopes and desires. I don't thank you enough. I could not have done this without you. Thank you from the bottom of my heart. I love you.

Introduction

"Who do you say that I am?" This was the opening line of a devotion that I had started in the beginning of 2015. I was given the gift of a *Charisma* magazine subscription by my dear friend Carol. On the cover of the January 2015 issue, there was mention of a twenty-one-day devotion with the Holy Spirit. I once again saw the Lord's perfect timing enter into my daily life. I had just completed my year-long Project 120. The time had come to sit down and begin writing the book. It seemed to me that there was no better way to begin the writing process than to take a few moments these first twenty-one days to interact with the Holy Spirit in a deliberate way through this devotion.

"Who do you say that I am?" When I read that question, everything got quiet around me, like it does when the Lord enters in and calls me to be still, to sit, and ponder. These are Holy moments I have come to be so thankful for; these are the moments when all the noise around me stops and His Presence is so palpable I can sit in that place for some time, sitting in awe of Him. Knowing He is so close literally

takes my breath away. The emotion I feel wells up, and I sit and bask in His Presence. After some time passes, He begins to speak to my heart.

As I've shared in my book *The Mustard Seed Chronicles*, I knew something was missing when I attended year after year of Bible study back in the '90s. I kept asking, searching, wondering what "it" was that I was searching after. I had come to know Jesus as my Savior, but I knew there was more. I could feel it in my bones. And God was faithful to me. In a moment, everything changed.

I wrote in my first book that meeting Jesus changed my life and He did, but the Holy Spirit was the key person that I had to fully relationship with and begin to know in order for my life to be complete in the saving Grace Jesus offers. Sure enough, my life dramatically transformed in August of 2000 when I encountered the Holy Spirit in a real, personal way. The Holy Spirit rocked my world to the core and I have not looked back.

I love the Holy Spirit. I have a passion for Him that is real and deep. My love for Him today far exceeds those early days of discovery with Him. Getting to know Him over these last fifteen years has been beyond anything I could have comprehended. The proverbial saying "This is just the tip of the iceberg" is true. I know I have only touched the surface of all of who the Holy Spirit is, and in this lifetime of mine, I am content and fully aware that I will not know all of His facets and ways and His beauty. But my passion for Him continues to grow and my passion for others to know Him grows as well. I am totally convinced that is one of the reasons He invited me in to Project 120. I am getting to share more about my admiration and wonderment for Him!

In the article in *Charisma* magazine, Jennifer LeClaire wrote from Holy Spirit's vantage point:

> *Jesus once asked His disciples, "Who do you say that I am?" Many people knew He was a great prophet, but only Peter received the revelation that He was the Christ, the Son of the living God. "Now, I ask you, who do you say that I am? Many people disregard My work in their lives because they don't understand who I am. And even those who know Me don't always have a continual awareness of My presence and a deep revelation of My love for them. Who do you say that I am? Search My heart, and I will show you a new realm of My faithfulness, My kindness, and so much more. Search My heart."*

Project 120 put me on a journey to search the heart of the Holy Spirit in a new way, and hopefully share His heart with others at the same time. Matthew 7:7 reminds us that when we seek Him with our whole heart, He will make Himself known. "Keep on asking, and you will receive what you ask for. Keep on seeking, and you will find.

Keep on knocking, and the door will be opened to you. For everyone who asks, receives. Everyone who seeks, finds. And to everyone who knocks, the door will be opened." (Matthew 7:7-8) My friendship with the Holy Spirit has become more real, more "normal," if you will. I now see the supernatural life of the Holy Spirit as a natural part of my daily life as my relationship with Him continues to broaden and expand.

There are no coincidences in life. This I have come to truly believe. Small, big, or seemingly irrelevant happenstances are all part of the Holy Spirit's intricate connection in our lives. Project 120 presented a wonderful time for me to hang out one-on-one with the Holy Spirit in a new way, and I am thrilled to have a chance to share some of those stories with you. My prayer is that you will desire more than ever to know the heart of the Holy Spirit. My deepest yearning is that you will want to invite Him into your life and desire to hear His Voice. And it is my most sincere hope that you will be willing to follow Him, so you will be able to answer Him clearly and with joy and excitement when He asks, *"Who do YOU think that I am?"*

Chapter 1

His Sheep Know His Voice

Project 120 was not my idea. It was the Lord's. And it all began on December 26, 2013.

Never in my life have I gone shopping at the mall the day after Christmas. I know it is a big day for sales, like the day after Thanksgiving, and I know people wait all year for those bargain days. Not me. By the time the holidays have come and gone, I am usually worn out and ready to rest. Shopping on that day had never sounded even remotely enjoyable to me.

However, I can't remember a time when I woke up the day after Christmas so rested and full of pep. Seeing all the sale ads reading the newspaper that morning made me think it might actually be fun to go out and see if I could find a good bargain. I was actually thinking ahead to the following Christmas and finding great presents for my prayer group, the Glory Girls, (a.k.a. the GGs). I had an idea of what kind of ornament I wanted to get them and had seen some at Belk. Since I needed to purchase about fifteen ornaments, it seemed like a good idea to pop over to the mall and check out whether they were now on sale.

I must say, I had a wonderful time. I found the exact ornaments I was looking for, plus a few extra goodies, all for 75 percent off! It was a successful trip and I was feeling good about my shopping spree as I walked toward the escalator to head home.

On my way, an African-American woman appeared in front of me and got on the escalator ahead of me. I first noticed her light-colored lavender corduroys. The back seam looked as if it had been resewn several times and the right back pocket was ripped, hanging on by a thread. She had on an old, soiled tan jacket, her hair was disheveled, and her very white Crocs shoes were hard to miss and looked to be at least one size too big.

Immediately, a thought came to mind. I had begun making it a habit to carry several Chick-fil-A gift cards with me to hand out to people who seemed to be in need; I would give one to her. As we rode up the escalator, I wondered how to approach her and what to say to bless her, all the while looking through my purse for one of the gift cards.

When we got to the third floor, she exited off the escalator ahead of me. I was still looking through my purse for a gift card when

I remembered I had emptied it out the night before. The gift cards were at home, sitting on my dresser! I began wondering if I should just offer a cash gift to her to bless her, again processing in my mind what that would look like and what I should say. When I finally looked up to approach her, trusting the right words would come at that moment, I realized she was nowhere in sight. I looked toward all four exits of the store to see if I could spot her, but there were no white Crocs and lavender cords anywhere.

In that quick moment, she was gone.

As I continued out of the department store to the parking lot, I began to wonder if maybe she had been an angel the Lord had put in my path to see what my heart's reaction would be. These occasions had been popping up more frequently as I had been asking—praying, really—to have more of a heart like the Father's. Up to this point, those moments to "love," whether it was giving money or a gift card, had all been done in secret, only known between me and the Lord. Little did I know He was getting ready to give me an opportunity to make this way of blessing people more purposeful.

Walking to my car, the Holy Spirit began to speak to me. John 10:27 says, "My sheep listen to my voice; I know them, and they follow me." He began telling me that my reaction to the woman on the escalator had been good. He said that I had responded with His heart and now He had a new opportunity He wanted me to be part of that would not only bless those He put in my path, but would be a blessing for me as well. I was intrigued and asked Him what His idea was.

On January 1, 2014, He said I was to buy ten ten-dollar Chick-fil-A gift cards. By the end of January, all ten were to be given away. I was to do this each month for the twelve months of 2014, giving away 120 gift cards to people He would put in my path. He went on to say that this would be part of the subject matter for my next book, and the title of the book would be *Project 120*.

I was surprised, excited, and a little bit nervous about this creative plan. It sounded like a brilliant concept, but I wondered if I could be faithful to keep up with it for an entire year. And yet my spirit jumped with joy at this idea, recognizing that God Himself was communing one-on-one with me about something that was on His heart, something different and unique, something that sounded so simple and yet could have long lasting effects and blessing. By the time I got to my car in the parking deck, I knew that all I had to do was say, "Yes, Lord, I am willing," and that is what I did. With that response to His proposal, Project 120 was conceived.

I continue to marvel at the Lord and His way of doing things. Here I was, minding my own business, shopping at the mall, not really thinking of anything spiritual or important when He interrupted, because it was time to begin a new adventure with Him. He is a master setter-upper, that's for sure. The idea that handing out 120 Chick-fil-A gift cards would be the flame that ignited a book is pretty creative, don't you think? It's marvelous how He operates. And what I have come to know is that this is how He desires to relationship with each one of His children.

As I drove home, I began to dream of what the year ahead would look like. Thoughts of Him intersecting my life with people I did not know sounded interesting and challenging. This idea of His was going to take me out of the shelter of ministering in my home prayer group, and send me out to share my faith in a way I was not so used to. It most surely was going to be an exercise to get me out of my comfort zone. But I also imagined there was going to be more to it than that. This invitation was also going to present an opportunity for me to tune my ear more purposefully to hear His "still small voice" (1 Kings 19:12) that I had been learning to hear and discern for over fourteen years. I was excited to move forward with this notion and watch Him create something Holy and unique out of a pretty simple idea and a pretty simple gesture of kindness and love.

When I got home from the mall, I told my husband Rob what had happened. His excitement at the idea added encouragement, and the next day, I went out and bought my first ten gift cards. The Lord's ways are higher and loftier than ours. I was eager to see how something so elementary would affect my life and others' in the year ahead.

Chapter 2

Missed Opportunities Can
Always Be Corrected

On January 1, 2014, we had no real plans other than to stay in, relax, and have a meal at home. We'd had a great time the night before ringing in the New Year with friends, having dinner at Dee Dee and Ed's. Although I had planned ahead and shopped for our New Year's night dinner, I still needed some things at the grocery store. So at noon, I headed out to the Harris Teeter up the street. As I entered the store, I suddenly heard the familiar voice of the Holy Spirit speak two words: *gift card*. My antennae immediately went up. I checked to make sure the gift cards were in my purse. They were. I was surprised that on Day One, I might be giving my first one away.

Walking around the aisles, I soon saw a young mom with her three small children, who were crawling in and out of a grocery cart. I asked, "Lord, do I give some of the gift cards away to them?" No response came, and I had no real sense in my spirit to do so, so I continued to walk around the store, discerning and wondering if I would run across someone to give a blessing to. I had no idea what this deliberate gift card giving was supposed to look like and I was probably overthinking it. I now know I was putting unnecessary pressure on myself, but I did not want to make a mistake, which is silly to even think. *How can giving a gift card to someone ever be a mistake?*

I ended up at the sandwich station to get a sub for my son Rob, and came upon an interesting scene. The lady ahead of me was being very rude to the lady making the subs. I was so taken aback by the customer's bad manners that I began praying quietly for the lady behind the counter. Her nametag read *Lisa*. When she finished making the sub to this woman's specifications, she wrapped it up, handed it to her, and the lady took it, walking off without so much as a thank you.

Lisa took a deep breath, wiped down the counter, and then looked up at me, asking what she could help me with.

"Happy New Year," I said.

"Happy New Year to you," she replied courteously.

"That lady wasn't very nice," I continued.

"Oh, she comes in here all the time and always acts that way," Lisa said matter-of-factly.

I told her I was sorry and gave her my order. When she was

done and handed the sandwich to me, I thanked her and told her to have a blessed afternoon. "I will," she replied and then with a smile, she said, "I went to church last night."

Assuming that comment meant she would be able to move on quickly from her rude customer, I headed to the self-checkout aisle, since my shopping was complete. I paid for my groceries, loaded up my food, got in the car and headed home. It was not until I was half-way home that the Holy Spirit gently spoke and said, "You just missed an opportunity to give away your first gift card." I immediately knew I should have given one to Lisa.

I drove the rest of the way home, thanking the Lord that He redeems. I told Him I would be willing to go back up to the Harris Teeter after lunch to give Lisa a gift card if that was His true desire. I began to sense that this gift card giveaway thing was going to be very interesting, especially if I missed the chance to give one away when I was supposed to. I got home, unloaded the groceries, and made lunch. After I ate, I cleaned up and then sat down to journal what had happened, when immediately I thought again of Lisa. The Lord will send you a nudge or two if He has something for you to do that you have not done. I knew better than to wait anymore. I was not going to miss out on this first opportunity. It was too easy to remedy. I told Rob what had transpired, hopped in my car, and drove back to the Harris Teeter.

When I got back to the store, Lisa was no longer at the sub-making station. I approached the lady who was now working behind the counter and asked if Lisa was still in the store. Sure enough, she was still at work, but was currently on her lunch break. I told the lady I had a little something I wanted to give to Lisa if she wouldn't mind taking me to where she might be, and without delay, this nice employee took me to the place Lisa apparently takes her daily lunch breaks—the stairwell.

Lisa was very surprised to see me. I told her I had a little God story to share with her, and without explaining the entire Project 120 idea, I briefly told her about the gift cards and how the Lord, on my way home from the store, had told me I had missed my first opportunity to give one away. I told her I was supposed to give one to her. She began crying so hard that I got teary-eyed as well. I told her that her reaction was confirmation to me that I was supposed to come back and bless her. She stood up and gave me a big hug as I handed her the gift card. "I'm going to hold on to this for a while," she said as she held it close to her chest. I told her it wasn't much, but I knew it was a sign for her, that the Lord wanted to bless her, and then I began to prophesy over her as the Holy Spirit prompted. I told her how much He cared for her and that 2014 was going to be a year when the provision in the storehouses of heaven were going to be released to her in new measure. She was so overcome with emotion that she could hardly talk. I don't remember what else I was led to say to her, but at the end, she simply nodded and said she agreed with me. She gave me another hug and I left. And that was it.

As I walked out of the store, I said out loud, "Lord, this is going to be one heck of fun adventure this year ahead!" Lisa's tearful reaction took me by complete surprise. In my mind, it was just a ten-dollar gift card. But the Lord knew that Lisa needed a blessing and the money amount did not matter. The action and gesture of kindness and love was what was important. He knew deep down how that gift of generosity would minister to her that day. And He knew I would have fun giving it. It's not really important that I know anything else about it. All I was being called to do was listen and give as He directed. What I have learned and once again experienced this day is that as long as we choose to listen to the still small voice and obey, missed opportunities can always be corrected.

I got in my car and drove back home.

One down, one hundred and nineteen to go.

Chapter 3

True Giving Has No Parameters.
It Simply Requires Perception and Love.

To my complete surprise, on January 4th, the Holy Spirit put three more people in my path to bless with the gift cards. Once again, I was at another grocery store when I noticed a cute young girl standing outside the store, holding a worn-out pink bucket. She was wearing a pink hoodie matched with some pink pants. I stopped to ask her what she was selling. She said she was not selling anything, but collecting money to buy new uniforms for her dance troupe. I noticed a small card table, which housed several trophies, ones that her dance troupe had won in past competitions. Her mom and older sister were standing beside the trophy table, letting this precious young one do the talking. I realize now I never asked her name, but did find out that she was in the third grade. I told her I would be happy to give a donation as soon as I got my shopping done. I promised I would come right back and she said, "Okay."

While in the store, I began to wonder if I should give one, two or three gift cards to this family? As I shopped, I thought that it would be a blessing for them to be able to go to a warm Chick-fil-A and have a good meal after standing outside in 25-degree weather, soliciting donations. Many times, but not always, the Holy Spirit gives me a "strong witness" when He is speaking to me about something important or urgent. It is hard to describe, but for me, when He really wants to make a point or confirm the accuracy of what I am hearing or saying or sensing, I get a physical quickening and a tightening in my gut. I've also been known to let out an involuntary verbal "Whoa" from time to time. The GGs are used to the ways the Holy Spirit manifests Himself in and through me. I know it is different and might sound a bit odd, but I have learned to embrace these demonstrations of the Spirit in me, and I no longer apologize for it or worry about what others may think.

As I headed to the checkout line, I saw that the precious young one had come inside and was looking for me. I caught her eye and told her I was almost done and would be out shortly. Again she said, "Okay," and headed back to her post. As I was waiting for my groceries to be bagged, I made the decision to give them three gift cards, plus a money donation for the dance uniforms.

When I headed out of the store, I put my donation in her pink bucket and then looked her in the eye and said that I wanted to bless her, her mom, and her sister with some Chick-fil-A gifts cards so they could go have lunch. Her eyes got as big as saucers and she pointed over to an old white car in the parking lot. "My mom is in the car," and with the understanding that I was to go give them to her mom, I was the one who now said, "Okay."

Her mom was getting out of the car as I approached. I told her I had been given an opportunity by the Lord to bless people with gift cards, and that I wanted to give her three so she and her daughters could get out of the cold and go and have a good lunch today. Tears welled up in the mother's eyes as I handed them to her. And again, as with Lisa, I got the biggest hug along with a "Thank you!" With that, I went to my car with my groceries and she went back to her post next to her daughters.

In the car, I began to question my decision of giving three gift cards away, when Holy Spirit quietly said, "It's good to be an extravagant giver, Anne." That quickly settled any concern I had. I was beginning to realize that I couldn't mess this thing up. True giving has no parameters. It simply requires perception and love.

Chapter 4

Being Obedient Is Fun

At the end of January, I had a dream. In the dream, I gave away five gift cards to one family. When I awoke from the dream, I realized that the gift cards had not even been on my mind. I went to count them, and I found I did have five left to give out. Several events were happening in my family that had suddenly taken a lot of my time, attention, and emotion. Now, with just a couple of days left in the month, I found myself questioning if I was going to be able to stick to the task at hand. I asked the Holy Spirit for help. I simply needed to believe He would direct me if indeed this really was an assignment He had called me to. I trusted that He would set me up as He had at the beginning of the month.

As my day unfolded, I kept thinking of my dream and wondering how giving away the last five cards was going to happen. I did not want to give them away just to give them away.

In the afternoon, my son Rob needed to be dropped off at a friend's house, as he was heading out of town for the weekend. I decided since I was close to downtown, I would go on and gather all the bags of clothes to be donated that I had piling up in the guest room and take them to Crisis Assistance Ministry after I dropped off Rob. As I was loading the car, the thought dropped into my mind that maybe I would have the opportunity to give the gift cards away at the Ministry.

I pulled up to the donation area to unload my bags, got my receipt and headed back out to the main street. I began asking the Lord to please show me if there was anyone nearby that I could give the gifts cards to. As I got closer to the main intersection, I noticed a car packed to the brim with stuff parked in the parking lot to my right. In a split second, I made a decision to turn right into the parking lot. I pulled my car in front of the car that was parked and I stopped. Rolling down my window, I saw a person was in the car—the back car door was open. I could not tell if the person sitting there was a woman or a man, so I loudly said, "Could you use a blessing today?"

"What?"

"Could you use a blessing today?" I repeated, and with that, a woman emerged from the car and came over to my open window.

"Yes, I could," she said.

"Would a couple Chick-fil-A gift cards help you?" I said, as she leaned in toward me.

"Oh yes, that would be such a blessing." And she reached out to take the two I offered.

"How many could you use?" I asked.

"Well, there are five of us," she answered.

And then I instantly knew. This was where I was supposed to be and to whom I was to give the last cards to.

"Well, that's exactly how many I have," I answered. "The Lord gave me a dream and in the dream, I gave all five of them away to a family, so I guess that's you!"

Tears started rolling down the woman's cheeks, and welling up in my eyes as well. In unison, we both said to one another, "What is your name?"

Then we both laughed.

"I'm Tonya," she said.

"I'm Anne. Isn't it amazing that the Lord gave me a dream that I would be handing out these five cards to a family? I am so blessed to meet you."

"Isn't it fun to be obedient?" she replied.

"Yes it is," I said in return. "Yes it is!"

I've continued to ponder the question she asked me: *Isn't it fun to be obedient?*

Obedience is what following Jesus is all about, and it *is* fun! Obedience is a core value of the Christian faith, and this gift-card giving exercise was showing me the joy obedience brings.

Scripture is full of lessons on obedience. Jesus shows us through His life what obedience looks like. "He only did what the Father told Him to do." (John 5:19) He was only interested in obeying His Father's ways and desires. He did not worry what others thought and He did not listen to other voices that did not line up with His Father's will. There are many other voices vying for our attention and we need to learn to discern what voices we are listening to. There is the voice of religion (the Pharisees' ways), there is the voice of our own soul (the way we want to do things), and there is the voice of the devil. Remember the temptation in the desert? (Matthew 4) Yep, the devil has a voice too. Being able to differentiate between the different voices that speak to us is paramount. We can know the Voice of the Lord. And when we learn to hear Him, we can then be obedient to His desires and ways for our lives.

When I read about the life of Jesus, I see that He only healed when the Father told Him to heal. He only taught when the Father told Him to teach. He only ministered when the Father told Him to minister. And when He was to go away and be alone with the Father, He obeyed. Jesus obeyed the Father even unto death. In His final hours, we read that Jesus asked the Father if the cup of the crucifixion could be taken from Him. "Father, if you are willing, take this cup from me; yet not my will, but yours be done." (Luke 22:42)

These Scriptures and others tell me that obedience will at times be very difficult and almost seem impossible. But that is not the end of the story! We see that resurrection and life came as a result of Jesus's obedience to His Father's Voice and the same comes to us when we are obedient too.

Being obedient allows us to show our love to the Lord. In John 14:15, Jesus says, "If you love me, you will obey what I command." We also show our love to the Lord when we love one another. John 13:34-35 says, "A new command I give you: Love one another. As I have loved you, so you must love one another. By this everyone will know that you are my disciples, if you love one another." Being obedient means we have to forgive. (Colossians 3:13) Being obedient requires patience. (Revelation 14:12.)

I am continuing to learn on this journey called Christianity about the importance of being obedient. Opening myself up to Him and learning to discern His Voice has drawn me deeper and deeper into obedience to Him and His ways. The blessings far outweigh the occasional discomfort, awkwardness, or even difficulty. His ways are always the best.

I know Tonya clearly experienced the impact and blessing of obedience that day. She told me that things were looking up for her— that she was going to be moving into a place of her own and out of her car soon. Before we could talk much longer, a car pulled up on the other side of her and someone called out to her. Abruptly, our conversation came to an end.

Tonya gave me a big hug through my car window, and thanked me again. As she walked over to the other car to chat, I said goodbye and drove away, shaking my head in awe of what had just quickly happened.

I am grateful that the Lord took care of setting me up to get those five cards to Tonya that day. I have thought of her often since that meeting and have believed that new opportunities and blessings would materialize for her. And I am thankful I was obedient to the nudge of the Holy Spirit that day, turning my car into that parking lot. Obedience IS fun, and it is rewarding as well.

Chapter 5

The Lord Is Good to Everyone

February came and went and, to be candid, the gift cards really were not on my mind. A lot of my time was being spent dealing with my aging parents and their upcoming move into a new apartment at a retirement community in Roanoke, Virginia. As a result, I was on the road every other weekend to help them out as their moving date drew near.

In 2003, my mom and dad moved out of the house I grew up in to downsize to a smaller home that was just around the corner. We'd since had years of discussion as to whether this would be their final home, or if a move to a retirement community would be best so they could be in a place where they could be taken care of if need be. Maybe for some, these kinds of decisions are easy, but not for my folks. Although they knew in their heads it might be the wisest decision to move, in their hearts the thought of this second move was proving to be even tougher than the first.

When my folks made their first big move, the Lord was ever present. Our family home on Allendale Street was beautiful and the neighborhood I grew up in was idyllic. There were enough girls in the neighborhood to have wonderful tea parties, Barbie get-togethers, and thanks to Marilyn Boardman and her trunk full of ball gowns and high-heeled shoes, we also had hours and hours of dress-up and make-believe parties and events. In the summer evenings, there were more than enough kids to have long games of kick-the-can, and in the winter, our street and the Crocketts' front yard were perfect locations for us to use our flexible-flyer sleds when it snowed, which it did all the time back then. Summertime and holidays were full of social times with other families; Christmas mornings were spent running back and forth between neighbors' homes to see what Santa had brought. Overall, growing up on Allendale Street had been so good, and I think that the memories of those good times kept my parents in that house much longer than they should have stayed there.

When a developer began building cluster homes nearby, several friends of my parents decided it was time to downsize. Suddenly, Southwood became the new hot spot for folks in their seventies. Conversations began and this process took on a life of its own. After years of talk and discussion with my parents, my siblings and I were convinced that a move would never happen. But sure enough, out of the blue, what seemed to look like a perfect house for them became available and both of my parents seemed interested. At this point, after so many years of talk, I found myself saying, "I will believe it when I see it," so I was shocked when I got a call from Mom one day saying they were actually talking about signing a contract.

The closer they got to signing the contract on the Southwood house, however, the more my phone began ringing, sometimes several times a day. Mom and Dad were suddenly finding little things wrong with the potential new house, and I could see they were slowly trying to back out of the move. I won't ever forget getting a call one Tuesday morning from Mom to tell me she and Dad did not think they could sign the contract. I immediately called my husband Rob at work to tell him what was happening and without hesitation he said, "Anne, we've got to get in the car and drive to Roanoke in the morning and help your mom and dad seal the deal." With the ease that comes only from Divine help, I was able to quickly secure our dear sitter Bobbie to stay overnight with our children Hallie and Rob, who were eight and six at the time, and early the next morning, we were in the car driving to Roanoke.

When we arrived at the Allendale Street home, Rob and I visited briefly with my folks before all of us headed to the South-wood house to check it out. As we were leaving, the phone rang and Mom decided to answer it. To our complete surprise, it was a local ophthalmologist, calling to say he had heard through the grapevine that Mom and Dad might be moving and selling their home, and wondered if that was true. When Mom said it was true, he then asked if he could please come see the Allendale Street house during his lunch break—that day. What? Mom said, "Come on over," and with some disbelief in the timing of the call, we headed to Southwood to check out this smaller home my parents were ready to back out of committing to.

When we got to the Southwood house, Rob and I couldn't believe it. It was perfect! All the living space was on one level, but there was a small sitting area, bedroom, and bathroom in a loft on the second floor for guests. It was spacious but not too big, and the windows looked out over a beautiful backyard / common area. Honestly, there was not one thing we saw that would make us think this would not be the best place for Mom and Dad to downsize to, and by the end of the walk-through, they recommitted and decided that it was a good decision and agreed they would sign the contract.

We then headed back to Allendale Street in time to meet the ophthalmologist. He liked the house so much he asked if he could come back and bring his wife with him at four that afternoon. I think my mom was in total shock when she got a call at six that evening with an offer on the house for the full asking price with no Realtor or inspection needed. In a matter of six hours, they had shown and sold the house on Allendale Street. We could hardly believe what was happening. Dad, Rob, and I decided we needed to go out and celebrate. Mom, however, was having a harder time with the news. She opted for a good cry and a large scoop of ice cream from Baskin Robbins. The next day, Mom and Dad signed the contract on the Southwood house and once they moved and settled in, they were content and thankful for their new home.

So when I'd visited my parents in Roanoke in the middle of January to help with some matters that were not at all house-related, I was in shock when my mom insisted we go out to the retirement community, Brandon Oaks, to look at a two-bedroom apartment that had become available. I was really taken aback when she said she liked it. For the last five years, this idea of moving to Brandon Oaks had been on the burner and I had several times accompanied them out there to look at different apartments. I have to admit that once again "I'll believe it when I see it" scrolled through my mind. But sure enough, it looked like five years of talking and processing and discerning about another move was possibly going to become a reality.

As we pulled away from the apartment at Brandon Oaks that day, the Holy Spirit spoke to me. He told me to take notice of the apartment number. It was apartment number 145. Then He suggested I look at Psalm 145. So that night, when things settled down and I got to my bedroom, I opened my Bible and began reading. Here are some of the verses that stood out:

The Lord is faithful to all his promises and loving towards all he has made. The Lord upholds all those who fall and lifts up all who are bowed down. The eyes of all look to you and you give them their food at the proper time. You open your hand and satisfy the desires of every living thing. The Lord is righteous in all his ways and loving towards all he has made. The Lord is near to all who call on him, to all who call on him in truth.

I don't know why I continue to be amazed at how the Lord loves on us so personally, sending a sign or an encouragement exactly when it is needed. If you don't know Him, if you don't know the sound of His Voice, you will miss these intimate hugs He so willingly gives.

Psalm 145 is full of God's Truth and promises to us, and when I read it that night, the verses above really spoke loudly to me. I could see that once again, the Lord's faithfulness to my parents was being revealed. The Holy Spirit nudged me the next morning to read Psalm 145 to my mom. I did. We both agreed that God's hand was on this new apartment for them. I knew in my heart that another repeat like what had happened eleven years ago was about to take place. Mom was so comforted by Psalm 145. The Lord was saying, "I've got this because it is the right time." And sure enough, He had a buyer waiting in the wings for the Southwood home.

Whether it is listening to His Voice about who to give a gift card to or simply listening and watching for Him to speak, maybe in an apartment number He puts right in front of you, one thing is for sure: He is able to inspire and give life as He provides what He knows we need. Even though my mind had not been on the gift cards, my ears were tuned in to the Holy Spirit's Voice. When we are willing to listen, He will surely lead the way and keep us in His timing.

So here I was on the last day of February, when I once again realized I had five cards in my purse to give away. I did not want to just give them away in order to meet the "deadline" of February 28. Sure enough, I still had them in my purse on March 1. That morning, as I headed to a local coffee shop to grab a coffee and a bite to eat before spending the entire day with my mom packing boxes, I ran into a man sharing his story with the barista. I listened as he told her that he was from Ireland and down on his luck. He was complaining about a tooth problem, talking about how he was all alone, not knowing anyone in Roanoke. As I waited for my order, the Holy Spirit gave me "the nudge" that I was now getting familiar with. I reached in my purse and pulled out the remaining five gifts cards. As I picked up my coffee and food to leave, I turned to him and said, "Excuse me, here is a blessing from the Lord for you today," and I handed him the five cards. He turned to me, looked at what I had given him and stared in disbelief, completely shocked. As I exited, he and the barista stood there, speechless. Neither of them said a thing.

I walked to my car and started getting tickled, wondering what in the world they thought of me. The more I thought of what they might be thinking and saying, the more I began to laugh. I don't know why I thought it was so funny, but I did. And I started laughing. I mean, I began laughing so hard, you know, one of those "I think I'm gonna wet my pants" kind of laughs, that I did not think I could drive safely back to Southwood. I had not had a good laugh like that in a long while. And I needed it! I began thanking the Lord. Truthfully, the stress and emotion that I had been experiencing dealing with this move my parents were making had taken more of a toll on me than I had realized. The blessing I gave away ended up blessing me in return, ushering in a release of healing balm for me that I did not even know I needed. It made me think of a Scripture in Luke 6:38: "Give, and it will be given to you. A good measure, pressed down, shaken together and running over, will be poured into your lap. For with the measure you use, it will be measured to you."

It's supposed to be enjoyable and childlike at times as we venture on in our day-to-day lives, listening to the Lord's Voice and following Him. I was thankful for a moment of laughter. And on this particular morning, driving back to my parents' to pack more boxes as they prepared for the move, I also could see in my mind's eye that the Lord was having a good laugh too.

Psalm 145

I will exalt you, my God and King,

and praise your name forever and ever.

I will praise you every day;

yes, I will praise you forever.

Great is the Lord! He is most worthy of praise!

No one can measure his greatness.

Let each generation tell its children of your mighty acts;

let them proclaim your power.

I will meditate on your majestic, glorious splendor

and your wonderful miracles.

Your awe-inspiring deeds will be on every tongue;

I will proclaim your greatness.

Everyone will share the story of your wonderful goodness;

they will sing with joy about your righteousness.

The Lord is merciful and compassionate,

slow to get angry and filled with unfailing love.

The Lord is good to everyone.

He showers compassion on all his creation.

All of your works will thank you, Lord,

and your faithful followers will praise you.

They will speak of the glory of your kingdom;

they will give examples of your power.

They will tell about your mighty deeds

and about the majesty and glory of your reign.

For your kingdom is an everlasting kingdom.

You rule throughout all generations.

The Lord always keeps his promises;

he is gracious in all he does.

The Lord helps the fallen

and lifts those bent beneath their loads.

The eyes of all look to you in hope;

you give them their food as they need it.

When you open your hand,

you satisfy the hunger and thirst of every living thing.

The Lord is righteous in everything he does;

he is filled with kindness.

The Lord is close to all who call on him,

yes, to all who call on him in truth.

He grants the desires of those who fear him;

he hears their cries for help and rescues them.

The Lord protects all those who love him,

but he destroys the wicked.

I will praise the Lord,

and may everyone on earth bless his holy name

forever and ever.

Chapter 6

The Lord Determines Our Steps

Up to this point in Project 120, I had been handing out gift cards to people I did not know. I had made it a habit in the beginning to write on the outside of each gift card envelope two things: On the line where it says "From," I wrote the Name "Jesus," and then on the amount line, I always put "$10.00," so the recipient would know how much money they had to spend on a meal. Because this entire idea was the Lord's, I felt compelled to make a statement of faith when giving the cards away. If I was not led to use Jesus's Name when talking and giving the card, the recipient would know who my Lord and Savoir was by reading what I had written on the envelope once they received it. And that was easy enough. So I was a bit taken aback at my own reaction when the Lord presented me with the opportunity to give a card out one day to someone who would recognize me.

Walking into the post office in early spring at the Park Road

Shopping Center, I was a caught off guard when the Holy Spirit whispered, *gift card*. As I continued down the hall, I could see several people waiting in line. You know the scene. It's not the friendliest place in the world. There's no real interaction with the others waiting in line to mail their packages, unless you see someone you know. You are just kind of standing there waiting . . . waiting. And I certainly don't think of the post office as a destination place people plan to go to in order to charitably give a gift to someone.

Sandy was the only one working behind the counter that morning, and I could tell by her countenance that her day had not started off well. As I waited for my turn to go to the counter, I was surprised by the battle of insecurities that began in my mind. *What will she think? Will the others in line hear me? What will THEY think? What if she does not receive it?* I was being called to step out a little further, and I must admit, I was wondering if I would ever be comfortable going back to this post office again if I stepped out in this way. I even began questioning if I was really hearing the Holy Spirit speaking to me.

Writing those words now sounds so silly to me, but at the time, I was nervous. The Lord seems to love to move us out of our comfort zones. It's part of being that ball of clay on the potter's wheel. (Isaiah 64:8) The Lord, if we are willing, will constantly mold us into the person He initially intended for us to be and use us as He sees fit.

When my time came to go up to the counter to mail my

package, I did not get so much as a smile or a look in the eye from Sandy. She simply began rolling off the series of questions she has to ask every time someone comes in to mail something. I dutifully answered. She weighed the package, I bought my stamp, and after the entire exchange was done, I took my step of faith.

I told her that the Lord had called me to bless certain people He put in my path and I felt He wanted me to bless her today, saying that she must be on His mind.

As I handed her the gift card, her entire countenance changed. "Thank you SO much," she said with a big, enthusiastic smile. And though that little ten-second exchange seemed so small, the Lord let me see the impact it had. To see her now engage me not only by looking me in the eye, but with a smile on her face and a word of thanks, I knew He had used that simple act to change the course of her day.

Thereafter, I had a minor shift in handing out the gift cards. Throughout the rest of the spring, I found that handing out cards to those who knew me was just as much fun as handing them out to strangers. From blessing the entire staff at my chiropractor's office to handing the cards out to waitresses and clerks in local stores and restaurants I frequent, I started to embrace this new method, and saw that I had to be flexible in how I approached and spoke to each person. No two recipients were the same in how they reacted. This made for a surprising, delightful walk with the Lord, and I knew more and more that that is exactly how He likes it to be!

As summer approached, my parents finally got moved into their new apartment. I had many more opportunities to hand out gift cards during my visits to Roanoke, which were still frequent. One time while in Roanoke, I surprised an entire crew at Starbucks by giving a card to each person working the early shift. I also was able to bless men and women working in Lowe's and Walmart, as we bought supplies there in order to put the finishing touches on Mom and Dad's new place. Each time, I got to see reactions of delight and thanksgiving.

During one of those Virginia trips, my husband Rob traveled with me, and he got to watch and see the exchange and smiles and hugs I received as a result. This made it extra fun. Rob has always been a huge supporter and encourager as my relationship with the Lord has grown. Though most of the time I handed these cards out while out on my own, it was a real joy to have him with me those times I gave in his presence.

My daughter Hallie returned home from her first year of college and my son Rob finished his junior year of high school. As the busyness of life took over, I got slack in keeping up with noting in my journal who I gave gift cards to. I began to worry about how I could relate my story to people if I did not have all the details written down. But The Lord, in His goodness, sent a Scripture along my path to remind me this was His work to do and He would show me the way.

Proverbs 16 reminded me He was in charge. All I had to do was be faithful to my assignment and He would take care of everything else.

To man belong the plans of the heart, but from the Lord comes the reply of the tongue. Commit to the Lord whatever you do, and your plans will succeed. In his heart a man plans his course, but the Lord determines his steps.

Proverbs 16:1,3,9

Project 120

Chapter 7

Trust the Lord in All of
Your Circumstances

With summer underway, the Holy Spirit began to change a few
more things. Up until this point, I had gone to the same Chick-fil-A
restaurant on Woodlawn Road to purchase my gift cards each month.
However, I felt prompted by the Holy Spirit to buy the rest of the
gift cards at the Chick-fil-A near Cotswold Mall, thus spreading the
blessing to another business, even though they did not know anything
about what I was doing. So dutifully, I changed my purchasing venue
and starting buying the gift cards at the new location, and did so for
the remainder of the year.

The other change happened when I got home from purchasing
those ten gift cards for the month of July. I was putting the gift cards
in their individual envelopes when the Holy Spirit spoke to my heart,
and said it was time to begin putting Scripture references on top of

each gift card. I liked the idea, and asked if there should be a theme, or if I was to look up my favorite verses. I got no immediate answer, so I started by using my favorite life verses for this next group of ten cards and did that for a couple of months.

After a couple of months, I was prompted to find Scriptures with the same theme—one month I referenced God's Glory, another month I used Scriptures about His Presence, and another, I mentioned words about His love for us. This exercise was yet another silver lining blessing for me, as I spent the beginning of each month in the Word, looking through verses to find just the right gem to put on a card, believing it would be a prophetic, life-giving word to the one who received it.

It is a real blessing to receive a prophetic word from someone. Prophecy is a gift of the Spirit the Lord tells us we should eagerly seek. (1 Corinthians 14:39) Prophecy, when correctly spoken with the Holy Spirit, "strengthens, encourages and comforts." (1 Corinthians 14:3) You will remember I mentioned the Lord had me speak words over Lisa, the first woman I gave a gift card to. Prophecy is a gift the Lord uses to show He is real! (1 Corinthians 14: 24-25.)

I remember one time a couple of years ago when I was invited to speak at a small prayer group meeting at a church. The Holy Spirit had me buy a puzzle and put different Scripture references on the back of each puzzle piece. As I opened my Bible, I invited the Holy Spirit to help me find Scripture to put on the back of each puzzle piece. I then prayed over the puzzle pieces, asking the Holy Spirit to give the right puzzle piece to the right person, hoping and trusting that the word on the puzzle piece would be a prophetic word to bless, encourage, or comfort the one who received it.

When the time came to hand out the puzzle pieces, I reminded each person that though we are each different, uniquely shaped and made, we are all part of God's puzzle, part of His master plan and purposes. And I remember each one being so touched by the words on their puzzle piece. Each person that morning responded positively to the word they received, saying that the word spoke directly to them. God is always in the details to show His children how much He cares for them, and can show His love even in something as small as a puzzle piece.

Putting the Scripture reference on the top of the gift card made me think I needed to change my usual delivery lines. I began talking a little more to each person I gave a card to, referencing the Scripture on top of the card and suggesting to the recipient that it might be a prophetic word for them. I encouraged them to go home and look up the Scripture on the card, trusting the Holy Spirit would then guide them to read on and see His Word open up. By this, I was implying and trusting that the Scripture was from the Lord Himself personally to the recipient. Again, each response was enthusiastic. Even though I was not led to keep up with who got what word, I truly believed each person received a word the Lord had in mind just for them.

One of the first cards I gave out with a verse on it was to a woman I ran into at a shopping center. I was running some errands and came out of a store when this very attractive woman, carrying a hot pink motorcycle helmet, walked by me. She was talking very loudly, actually yelling, at someone she was on the phone with. She was visibly upset and madder than a hornet. She ended up walking into a store as I entered a different one, all the while still on her phone, shouting. I was a bit embarrassed for her, and I wondered what in the world she was dealing with, when the Holy Spirit interrupted my train of thought and said He wanted me to give her a gift card.

I was not sure how in the world that could happen, so I finished my shopping thinking no more about it. I left the store and walked to my car. On my way to the parking lot I noticed a beautiful pink motorcycle parked several spaces down from my car on the other side of the median. The Holy Spirit quickened my spirit. I looked around and did not see the woman anywhere. I was not feeling led to try to track her down. And I was not feeling so comfortable about it anyway after overhearing her on the phone; I knew she was having a bad day and was not at all sure she would respond positively to me.

Whew, I thought. *I'm off the hook on this one.* I buckled my seat belt, turned on the car, ready to drive off. But I couldn't.

As I sat there, I realized that I was in a place where I needed to do exactly what the Lord was asking me to do. I was not feeling content about blowing this possible assignment off, so I said, out loud, "Lord, I am willing. Here's what I'll do. I am going to back out of this parking space, drive to the end of this row and make a U-turn back down to the next parking lane where the motorcycle is parked. If You really want me to talk to this lady, she's going to need to be somewhere in sight, or I am heading home." Sounds a little brazen, I know, but I was apprehensive. Having an encounter with this loud and angry woman was a big step for me and I was uneasy. I am not the kind of person who yells and curses at someone on my phone, in public or at home. I am not even comfortable talking on my phone in public at all. And I am not the type of person who gravitates toward a person who is yelling on their phone in public. Me—I go the other way!

By now, I am sure you can guess what happened. As I headed out of my parking space and made the U-turn to head back toward the stores and the motorcycle, the woman, with her hot pink helmet in hand, was indeed crossing the street toward the sidewalk to the pink motorcycle. Only God!

Here goes nothing. I pulled up alongside the motorcycle and stopped my car. Rolling down my window on the passenger side, I leaned over the seat and yelled, "Ma'am!"

She looked right at me with no real reaction. I continued. "The

Lord wants me to bless you today."

"Did you hear me?" she asked, and I realized she was referring to her earlier phone conversation.

"Yes, I did," I replied.

She made her way over to my car. I was parked halfway in the street, but not one vehicle came by us during this exchange. God really does know how to set something up.

"I am going through a very bitter divorce right now," she said with sadness and pain in her eyes.

With no hesitation, I said, "Well, I am here to tell you to stand strong. I am here to tell you that the Lord is with you." I extended my hand to her with the gift card and took notice, one of the few times I ever did when handing them out, to see what the Scripture was on the card. It read "Isaiah 55." Isaiah 55 is a beautiful invitation the Lord extends to the reader to come into His Presence so He can encourage, bless, and renew. This woman was so touched. There was humility and tenderness in her face. I watched tears well up in her eyes when she took the gift card.

Up to this point, I still had my sunglasses on. I reached up and took them off my face and looked her square in the eyes. "The Lord is with you. You stand firm and stand strong." The Holy Spirit was giving me words of comfort and reassurance to share with her in this difficult time. You could see visibly how they ministered to her. She nodded her head as a simple gesture of appreciation. I put my sunglasses back on my face, put the car in gear, and drove off.

I prayed for that woman the rest of the day. I couldn't get her off of my mind. A Pastor once said to several of us in a small group setting that he viewed intercession as a "boring gift of the Spirit." He could not have been more wrong! Praying for others, touching their lives with intercession is one of the most amazing ways the Lord uses us to bless others.

Father God created heaven and earth. He sent His Son Jesus to save us from our sin, to reconcile us back to the Father. Jesus then left and sent the Holy Spirit to empower us to advance His Kingdom here on earth. We CANNOT be about the Lord's business here on earth without the Holy Spirit leading, guiding, and directing us. We simply can't! It's impossible.

I can sit here and suppose all kinds of scenarios about why the Lord picked that woman to touch that day. Out of nowhere, the Lord showed up to tap her on the shoulder and remind her that He was with her, that He loved her, that He knew what was going on and He wanted her to be encouraged in that very rough place she was in.

In the meanwhile, I got to experience His invitation to enter into an exchange that did make me nervous initially, but in the end, allowed me to walk in my identity. Because I know he has wired me to pray for others, He used me that day to pray for her. When you get to operate in your identity, it is not only liberating, but gratifying as well. There is nothing more fulfilling than to see your own hands and feet used to glorify Him and His Kingdom.

I'm going to end this chapter with some of the Scriptures I put on the gift cards. My hope is the Lord will bless *you* with a word today. Trust Him in all of your circumstances: your joys, your trials, your hopes, your sorrows, and your fears. He sees you, He knows you, He cares for you, and He is with you, always. And He is able to take care of it all.

Love the Lord your God with all your heart and with all your soul and with all your strength. These commandments I give to you today are to be upon your hearts. Impress them on your children. Talk about them when you sit at home and when you walk along the road, when you lie down and when you get up. Tie them as symbols on your hands and bind them on your foreheads. Write them on the doorframes of your houses and on your gates.

Deuteronomy 6:5-9

And everyone who calls on the name of the Lord will be saved.

Acts 2:21

See what great love the Father has lavished on us, that we should be called children of God! And that is what we are! The reason the world does not know us is that it did not know him.

1 John 3:1

But you are a chosen people, a royal priesthood, a holy nation, God's special possession, that you may declare the praises of him who called you out of darkness into his wonderful light.

1 Peter 2:9

The Lord replied, "My Presence will go with you, and I will give you rest."

Exodus 33:14

Taste and see that the Lord is good; blessed is the one who takes refuge in him.

Psalm 34:8

Forever, O Lord, thy word is settled in heaven.

Psalm 119:89

You are the light of the world. A town built on a hill cannot be hidden. Neither do people light a lamp and put it under a bowl. Instead they put it on its stand, and it gives light to everyone in the house. In the same way, let your light shine before others, that they may see your good deeds and glorify your Father in heaven.

Matthew 5:14-16

Now may the Lord of peace himself give you peace at all times and in every way. The Lord be with all of you.

2 Thessalonians 3:16

Now may the God of peace, who through the blood of the eternal covenant brought back from the dead our Lord Jesus, that great Shepherd of the sheep, equip you with everything good for doing his will, and may he work in us what is pleasing to him, through Jesus Christ, to whom be glory for ever and ever. Amen.

Hebrews 13:20

Call to me and I will answer you and tell you great and unsearchable things you do not know.

Jeremiah 33:3

As the heavens are higher than the earth, so are my ways higher than your ways and my thoughts than your thoughts. As the rain and the snow come down from heaven, and do not return to it without watering the earth and making it bud and flourish, so that it yields seed for the sower and bread for the eater, so is my word that goes out from my mouth: it will not return to me empty, but will accomplish what I desire and achieve the purpose for which I sent it.

Isaiah 55:9-11

Chapter 8

Giving Is Kindness in Its Truest Form

Project 120 has not only been a project about pressing in to hear the "still small voice" of the Holy Spirit. It has also been an exercise to see the effect and the power of giving. So I want to take a minute to reflect on the power of giving.

Giving is a kindness in its truest form and it is unselfish when it comes from the heart. All of us were created to love and all of us were created to reach out to others with generosity, compassion, and good intention. The Father gives in abundance: He gives His grace, He gives His mercy, He gives us compassion, and He gives us His love. And the Father gave to us the most powerful and life-altering gift of all, His one and only Son. Whoever believes in Him will have eternal life. (John 3:16) Giving is the very nature of the Lord and since you and I are His children, giving is in our very nature too.

Many years ago, the movie *Pay It Forward* was released. It is the story of a young boy who was challenged by his teacher to go out into the world and pick three people to demonstrate an act of kindness toward. Sounds pretty simple. Kind of like handing out Chick-fil-A gift cards. The movie chronicles how one act of kindness created a movement of paying it forward, and it showed how acts of kindness not only blessed those who received but also blessed those who did the giving.

I imagine every person who reads *Project 120* has stories of their own they can share about times they've extended kindness to someone else. This idea to give out 120 gift cards was a clear plan and opportunity the Lord gave me in 2014, but I want you to pause for a moment and be still. Let the Holy Spirit remind you of all the acts of giving and kindness you have displayed in recent weeks and months and years. I would bet that some of you have taken a meal to a friend who was suffering a loss. Some of you, I imagine, have reached out to a person who needed a sympathetic ear, because you learned they received a bad medical report and you could relate. Some of you have been in a grocery store checkout line and given extra money to the person in front of you when you realized they did not have enough money to pay for their groceries. Some of you have taken a walk with a friend because they were lonely. Some of you have donated blood at a blood drive and others have donated hours each week to under-privileged kids. Some of you have flown halfway across the country to support a family member. I don't know what it looks like in your life but I know you have stories too. You may never write a book about the giving you have participated in or the kindnesses you have extended, but what is most important is that you gave and God sees it all.

I can still remember certain meals friends brought to me when my children were born. I don't think there is any greater gift than taking a meal to a new mom! I also remember the acts of kindness I received when I was diagnosed with melanoma and had to have surgery on my ear. The words of encouragement, the flowers, the "drop-ins" by friends, all helped and blessed us in a time when we really needed some TLC.

Deuteronomy 15:10 says, "Give generously to him and do so without a grudging heart; then because of this the Lord your God will bless you in all your work and in everything you put your hand to." Giving actually has a gift that comes back to the giver: God's blessing! And that too can take on many shapes and forms. I have found that I am blessed with pure joy when I give. There is no better feeling in the world.

So whether it's something big like raising money for a charity or the gift of your time to support someone in need or the smile you give to the stranger in a parking lot, enjoy the acts of giving and kindness you have extended to others. "This service that you perform is not only supplying the needs of God's people but is also overflowing in many expressions of thanks to God." (2 Corinthians 9:12) And if you never have an opportunity to tell others about your kind acts, don't worry about that. When our giving comes from our heart, it's not about letting others know and getting their approval. It's simply about being who we are created to be and following the nudge the Holy Spirit gives, so we can be His expression of love, kindness, and grace; so we can be His Hands and Feet in a broken world.

Chapter 9

There Is an Extra Blessing for the One Who Goes Back and Says Thank You

In September, several of the GGs went away for a long weekend to a conference at a church in Corinth, Texas, Glory of Zion. GOZ is a ministry the Glory Girls have been connected to and aligned with for many years now. Chuck Pierce is the Apostolic leader of GOZ. He has a father's heart for the Body of Christ like no one else I know, and it is a place where authentic Christianity functions. The Spirit of Freedom operates there as the church purposes to hear what the Holy Spirit says as they choose to follow Him only. Few places compare, and the fruitfulness of the ministry at GOZ is undeniable.

Every September, Glory of Zion hosts a conference called "Head of The Year." For several days, speakers from all over the globe come and prophetically share revelation the Lord has shown them for the year ahead. "The Lord does nothing without first revealing it to the

Prophets." (Amos 3:7) I could write many a book on all GOZ has meant to me personally and to our prayer group, and what we have learned from them. It's too much to even try and delve into here, but I would highly recommend you take time to go to www.gloryofzion. com and tap into all this God-ordained ministry has to offer if you have any desire at all to further your faith with Father, Jesus, and the Holy Spirit.

While in Texas, the Holy Spirit had me hand out two of the gift cards. It was Saturday night and I was with several of the GGs heading back to the conference for the evening session. When we arrived at the GOZ property, we were surprised to see the same parking lot attendant who had been there earlier in the day waving us back into a parking place. He was beet red from being outdoors all day in the Texas sun, and looked exhausted. We were running kind of late and had to park a ways away, and as we were walking in, the Holy Spirit gave me my first assignment.

We got into the building where the conference was being held, found several seats together and once I was settled, I got a gift card and headed back out to the parking lot.

It was a beautiful, picturesque Texas night. The sky was pink and red as the sun was setting. It was warm, but not so hot that you couldn't stand it. The air was calm and all was quiet as most everyone had already arrived and were now inside. I headed to where we initially had seen the parking attendant when we arrived, and as I got closer, I saw him standing there, all alone, next to some parked cars.

I approached him and told him that our group had noticed him earlier that morning and I asked if he had been out there all day. He answered, "Yes," and I then asked him if there were any Chick-fil-A restaurants in Corinth. I realized at that moment I really had no idea if Corinth even had a Chick-fil-A. He said they did, that one was actually right down the road, so I continued, saying, "The Lord has sent me out here tonight to bless you. I can't imagine what a hard job this is when a conference is going on here, but the Lord really wants you to know that He sees you, He knows you are here, and He appreciates all you are doing. I have a gift card I want to give to you from Him as a thank you and I hope it blesses you. There is a Scripture written on top of the card. It may be a word for you." I handed him the card.

He appeared to be blown away. His smile went from earlobe to earlobe and he was so thankful and appreciative of the gift and the words. I had a sense that the gesture had really blessed him. I strolled back to the conference building to enjoy a night of worship and an amazing message from Dutch Sheets.

But that wasn't the only one the Lord had His eye on.

Throughout the entire conference weekend, there was one woman who stood out in the hallway where four halls intersected; her job was to direct the human traffic flow. Five sessions a day, morning, noon, and night, she was there, directing thousands of people, whether it be to the bookstore, the dining hall, the amazing Israel garden outside, the prayer tower. (That's just to name a few of the places we could go during breaks.) I had noticed her the entire time we had been there and she was always smiling, always pleasant, and always standing! So when the session ended Saturday evening, I was almost shocked to see her, still on duty, with a huge trash bag in hand going through the rows of chairs, picking up trash.

There were about ten of us who had managed to sit in a common area and we were taking our time collecting our things. Once again, the Holy Spirit quickened my spirit. I had one gift card left for the month, and it looked like she was supposed to be the recipient.

I grabbed the card and headed up to greet her. She looked worn out and appeared to be focused on getting stuff picked up. I almost hated to interrupt her because I knew she was probably ready to go home.

I approached her and in order to get her attention, said, "I want to bless you." She stopped what she was doing and looked at me. I continued. "I want you to know that I have noticed you. I have seen you here all day, every day since this conference began. And the Lord wants you to know that He has noticed you too. You might wonder if what you are doing is important. What you have been doing has been very important and I wanted to thank you for all you've done and make sure you know you have not gone un-noticed. The Lord wants to thank you as well, so here." And I handed her the gift card. "There is a Scripture at the top of the card. It may be a word for you for today or the year ahead." The woman dropped the trash bag and gave me a big hug. Her eyes teared up and she just looked at me and I looked at her, no words being said. For what seemed to me to be a couple of minutes, time stood still. And then, the Holy Spirit turned the tables on me. She began to speak:

"Just like the one leper who turned around and came back to thank Jesus for healing him, you are like him, and you will be blessed, Anne of North Carolina"—(I had a name tag on with my name and state)—"because you came back to say thank you. ALL you have received while you are here, all the words spoken and all the revelation released, you will take those words back to North Carolina."

At this point, I had gotten myself into my usual posture when receiving a word. I was standing still with both hands open as if receiving a gift, looking her right in the eye. She continued speaking other blessings over me that I could not remember once I got back to my seat to try to write it all down, but as she was speaking, she started slapping the palms of my hands saying, "Everything! Everything! Everything! Everything, Anne of North Carolina, that you have received here you are taking back to North Carolina. Your family will be blessed and your marriage will be blessed and the families and the marriages in North Carolina will be blessed and they will be restored. I say to you, you will carry back to North Carolina everything you received here and you will release it because you are the one who turned around and came back and said thank you."

Remembering this ambush the Lord had for me blesses me once again now as I write. I looked again at the story she was referencing, which is found in Luke 17:11-19:

> *Now on his way to Jerusalem, Jesus traveled along the border between Samaria and Galilee. As he was going into a village, ten men who had leprosy met him. They stood at a distance and called out in a loud voice, "Jesus, Master, have pity on us!" When he saw them, he said, "Go, show yourselves to the priests." And as they went, they were cleansed. One of them, when he saw he was healed, came back, praising God in a loud voice. He threw himself at Jesus's feet and thanked him—and he was a Samaritan. Jesus asked, "Were not all ten cleansed? Where are the other nine? Has no one returned to give praise to God except this foreigner?" Then he said to him, "Rise and go; your faith has made you well."*

I see such a clear picture in this passage, a clear picture that we all should all take hold of. When we call out to the Lord, He responds.

And when He speaks, we need to listen and obey. His words are life and they heal. And when we hear Him, we should acknowledge Him by giving Him thanks and praise.

That was the only time all year handing out the gift cards that someone turned around and extended a blessing back to me. The Holy Spirit does have creative ways of blessing us all, and I give thanks again today for that precious woman and the life words she spoke over me. There *is* an extra blessing for the one who goes back and says thank you.

Chapter 10

Limitations Come When We Are Unwilling to Hear His Voice and Follow Him

Throughout Project 120, I have learned more and more about being flexible, being willing, and being open to The Lord and His ways to use these gift cards as a way to touch and bless people. But I found, as I began to get closer to the end of the year, I wanted to be even more intentional in giving them out. Watch what you ask for!

Early one morning, I went to get a coffee before going to my chiropractic appointment. The line at the Starbucks was so long, I decided not to wait. I went to get adjusted and then headed back to the Harris Teeter, which houses a Starbucks, so I could enjoy a coffee while I shopped.

Cruising through the grocery aisles, sipping on my mocha, I passed a woman unloading boxes to restock Cheez-It and other products on the cracker aisle. I said, "Hi," as I passed her and went to the next aisle. No sooner did I turn the corner than the Holy Spirit softly spoke, "Give her a gift card." I continued pushing my cart and responded, "Are you sure?" If I had a dollar for every time I asked that question those months, I'd have a nice little savings saved up. The Holy Spirit said no more and I knew I needed to turn back around. I'd been shopping and passing people all over the store, so if He spoke to me when I passed her and asked me to share a gift card, I knew I just needed to be obedient.

Once again, I headed back to the aisle that I had just gone down to pass the woman for a second time. As I approached her, I interrupted her work and said, "This may be a little odd to you, but I am really trying to press in to hear the Lord's Voice and do what He says, and I am supposed to bless you today and give you this gift card. On it is a Scripture that may be a word for you today. You just test it and see."

And sure enough, the tears welled up in her eyes and she said, "Thank you!" No one was around us as this exchange occurred, and since she did not engage me any more in conversation and I did not feel led to say anything, I responded with, "You are welcome. Have a blessed day," and I headed to the checkout counter. That was easy. Short and sweet. Mission accomplished.

Once in line at the checkout counter, talking to the lady scanning my groceries, the Holy Spirit spoke to me again: "Go ask her if she has a prayer request." I immediately knew He was talking about the lady I had just given the gift card to. I was taken aback, as I was trying to have a conversation with the checkout lady and listen to the Holy Spirit at the same time. His suggestion was really making me uncomfortable. I sort of zoned out, thinking about what was happening in this moment, and the checkout clerk finally got my attention as I forgot I had asked for cash back from using my debit card. As she handed the money to me, I asked if it would be okay to leave my groceries there for a minute. I told her I needed to go ask someone on one of the aisles a question. She said, "Sure," and off I went for a third time, back to the cracker aisle to find the lady there still alone stocking the shelves.

"Okay," I said approaching her again, "this is obviously a Divine appointment because the Lord wanted me to come back over here to you and ask you if you have anything specific on your mind that I can pray about for you."

Again tears welled up in her eyes and she replied, "I'm getting married."

I was surprised at her response and even more surprised at what then came out of my mouth. "Are you and your fiancé spiritually aligned? Because if you are not, you need to address that before you get married."

More tears. And more confirmation this was the Lord at work as she began shaking her head, "No."

I found myself sharing with her the importance of being spiritually aligned with her husband. I told her that Rob and I had not been spiritually aligned when we first got married. I went on to say that marriage can be difficult at times and when there is no spiritual alignment, it can make things even more difficult. I explained that spiritual alignment is a key issue and if it is addressed early on, a lot of heartache down the road can be avoided.

I really couldn't believe all that I was saying and the boldness with which I was saying it! But the entire time I spoke, she nodded her head in agreement and I thought, *This really must be God and this really must be a weighing issue for her, because she seems more sad than happy and she seems to be agreeing with everything I am saying.*

After my little spiel, I asked, "When are you getting married?"

"The twenty-second," she replied.

"This November twenty-second?" I said, almost in shock.

"Yes," she answered.

Then I was really in awe of this Divine moment. The wedding was in a couple of weeks, and this woman was not a joyous bride-to-be. I quite frankly did not know what to do or say next, so I asked her if I could pray and she said, "Yes."

The two of us closed our eyes and I began to pray, "Father, bless this marriage I pray in Jesus's Name. Lord, this really must be on Your heart today for you to have me come back and talk with my sister. I ask that You please spiritually align this couple in Jesus's Name, that they would be willing to do the hard work now to address any spiritual issues so that they will be in right alignment with You and Your will as they begin their new life together. I ask these things in Jesus's Name."

The prayer seemed to touch her deeply. When we opened our eyes and I asked her what her name was.

"Michelle," she said.

"I'm Anne. Is there anything else?"

"No," she replied.

"Well, I guess this really must be on the Father's heart today for Him to have me come here to the store this morning to give you a word and blessing. He's got you and your fiancé in the Palm of His Hand, Michelle. Please know that I will be praying for you these next couple of weeks. I want you to expect a shift to happen. It will be okay. It will all be okay. What the enemy might have meant for harm, you know the Lord is now turning it to good."

My boldness and the words surprised me again, yet I knew it was the Holy Spirit moving in and through me. Michelle nodded her head in agreement, thanked me again, and gave me a hug. And that was that. I left her there to ponder all that had just happened, and I went, grabbed my groceries, and headed home.

My prayer for these last gift cards to be given out with

intentionality was already being answered. It can be a bit astonishing when the Holy Spirit gives you a direct word to speak to someone. When you learn to hear His Voice, He is able to use you in a multitude of ways. When you can hear His Voice, He is not limited to what He can share through us. The only limitations come from us and our unwillingness to participate with Him in what He asks us to do.

I don't know if I will ever see Michelle again. I have looked for her and probably will continue to look for her as I shop at that Harris Teeter. I have to believe that if the Lord touched such a personal issue with her that day, it was something that she needed to be encouraged to talk about with her fiancé. I am trusting that His higher, deeper, magnificent ways for the resolution were released that day for her, and I have to trust He will see it to completion.

I've also come to know that the Lord loves to confirm those things He calls us to be part of that might seem out of the box. Later that day, Connie, one of the Glory Girls, called to check in. She wanted to thank me for a birthday card I had given her. She then was led to read the Scripture to me that was on the card, Acts 22:14. When I heard numbers, I immediately saw in my mind's eye Michelle's wedding date—November 22, 2014! The Lord had my undivided attention. Truly, you can't make this stuff up. Acts 22:14-15 says, "Then he said: 'The God of our ancestors has chosen you to know his will and to see the Righteous One and to hear words from his mouth.

You will be his witness to all people of what you have seen and heard."

Supernaturally, I saw that the Lord was confirming to me what had taken place with Michelle. He had chosen her to know His will. He allowed her to see the Righteous One and hear words from His mouth. He simply used this gray-haired woman to be His mouthpiece. I have to believe Michelle testified to what happened that day, as I am now, being a witness to what we both experienced. This word was not only for her, but for me too, to encourage me as I step out more, releasing words I am led to share with others.

I don't think I will ever be immune to the supernatural ability of the Lord. When events like this happen, it personally moves me into a place of amazement and thanksgiving. I was once again blown away at His detailed, precise touch and His Love that He is so open to give to anyone who is willing to deliver a touch from Him and also to those who are open to receiving them.

Project 120

Chapter 11

Creation Is Moaning for Our Liberation

I ran across Romans 8:18-21 in a devotion I was reading that gave me cause to pause.

> *I consider that our present sufferings are not worth comparing with the glory that will be revealed in us. For the creation waits in eager expectation for the children of God to be revealed. For the creation was subjected to frustration, not by its own choice, but by the will of the one who subjected it, in hope that the creation itself will be liberated from its bondage to decay and brought into the freedom and glory of the children of God.*

When I finished reading those verses, something happened. It was like the Holy Spirit pulled back a veil. I suddenly saw a new meaning in those verses for the very first time. This is what I was seeing and understanding: even though there are things we might be presently suffering through, those sufferings are nothing compared *to the glory that is in us to be revealed.* And not only that, creation is waiting with great expectation, actually moaning for this happening because creation itself will be liberated from the bondage it has been in as the children of God finally come into their glory in Jesus. Creation is waiting for us to be who it is God created us to be!

I love it when hidden treasure is found in the Word. It gives me a deeper sense of reverence as I realize how profound and mysterious the written Word is. Let no one be mistaken. The Word of God is alive. It is active and alive, sharper than any two-edged sword, and it cuts between the bone and marrow. (Hebrews 4:12) In 2 Timothy 2:9, it says, "The word of God is not chained." I love that! The Word of God is not confined to our way of looking at it; it is not bound by our thoughts and understanding. The Word of God is full of life and none of us will ever find all the hidden mystery that is tucked in the Word, but aren't we blessed to have the freedom to mine the Word so we can to find the gems that are there to be discovered? It's the greatest treasure hunt we have access to, and it will continue until Jesus comes back. When I find a nugget of revelation I have not seen before, I have to tell you, for me, there is nothing more intriguing or Holy.

So creation itself is waiting for the glory in us to be revealed.

What does that really mean, and what does that look like for you and for me? For many years now, I have listened to multiple teachings and read many books to help me understand my true identity. And you know what I've found? It all boils down to seeing myself the way God sees me. It all comes down to understanding how much He loves me and how much He values me. Scripture tells us that the Lord fearfully and wonderfully made us (Psalm 139:14). We are the apple of His eye. (Psalm 17:8). We are His delight and He rejoices over us. (Zephaniah 3:17) We are His masterpiece! (Ephesians 2:10) When I finally began to renew my mind and see myself the way God sees me, and *believed* these Truths, it caused a major shift in the way I saw myself. I think this is what sanctification really is: renewing our minds so we can see ourselves the way the Lord does. And when that happens, new confidence arises. When new confidence arises, a peace and security and an assurance begins to bloom and we begin to act more like Him. As a result, we can then go out and be real ambassadors for the Lord. For me, Project 120 was an avenue that encouraged me to be more and more of myself with myself and with those whose paths I crossed.

As my journey of being who it is the Lord has created me to be continued, I found myself once again at the Harris Teeter giving a gift card to another shelf stocker, this time a man. He ended up surprising me. He was intrigued by my gesture and began asking me questions like "How did this all come about?" and "How have people responded?" He is the only person during this entire process who engaged me in conversation about what I was doing. And as a result, I revealed a bit about myself with him. I answered his questions and shared with him a little about who I was, telling him that I loved the Lord and that this exercise in handing out the gift cards was fine-tuning my hearing His Voice. He commented that his wife and I would get along, that it sounded like I was a lot like her. He said she loved to bless people too and that he was going to give the gift card to his wife so she could give it away, commenting that this kind of giving away a blessing to someone was right up her alley.

Those few moments with him were unexpected. I found myself appreciating being engaged in conversation on a more personal level. I am a giver by nature. Anyone who knows me well knows I love to do things for other people. One of the most active and daily ways I give is being a listener. I enjoy giving my time and my ear to others to be a support to them, to listen to them so I can encourage them and pray with them, especially if those who need an ear are hurting in some way. It brings a deep joy and sense of purpose when I am able to be there for others when they need someone to hear them.

I've learned I also enjoy sharing my faith. When *The Mustard Seed Chronicles* was first published in 2011, I was invited to share about the book with many different women's prayer groups. That was the first time I had been invited to speak and share my testimony.

Revelations 12:11 says, "And they overcame him (the devil) by the blood of the Lamb, and by the word of their testimony." Sharing our testimony has power. I find I can really relate more personally to another person when I hear them share their life story, don't you? Our testimony can also reveal different facets of the Lord to others who may or may not know Him. I've found that I enjoy sharing my faith journey with others as much as I love listening to others share theirs with me. So this particular day, I appreciated being asked to share my story of how the giving of gift cards came about.

All of this reminds me once again that we are His chosen ones. He has plans and purposes for each one of us. (Jeremiah 29:11) He deeply wants us in fellowship with Him and in relationship with Him AND with each other, and He wants us to know His Voice. Knowing how He sees us and being able to hear Him speak to us helps us function in our true identity. I pray that today you can see the undeniable Truth about who you truly are. You are one of God's treasures. And He loves you with an everlasting love. (Jeremiah 31:3) If you have struggled with seeing yourself through His eyes, and have struggled to hear His Voice, pray this prayer out loud right now. I trust the Holy Spirit will begin to reveal to you what a precious gem you are, and I trust Him to help you renew your mind so you can be all it is He created you to be.

Prayer:

Father, I come before You and ask that You bless me
right now with Your Presence.

Holy Spirit, come.

Breathe new life on me I pray in Jesus's Name.

Circumnavigate all the junk that has gotten in the way
to distract, to rob, to steal, to destroy, to keep me
from understanding how precious I am to You.

I am asking that You bless me with a fresh
understanding of who I am in You.

I pray that the veil on my eyes will be removed so I can see
the true value of who I really am.

I pray I can know Your Truth regardless of untruths
spoken to me, by me or about me,
untruths that have not been life giving.

Your Word, Lord, trumps all lies and wrong beliefs.

The thief comes to steal and kill and destroy;
YOU come that I may have life,
and have it to the full! (John 10:10)

Renew my mind today.

Come Lord Jesus and make Yourself known to me in a new way.

And Lord, I want to hear You.

I am Your child and I know you speak to me.

Help me discern Your Voice.

Help me recognize Your Voice.

Confirm to me that I am hearing You.

Another voice I do not want to follow.

Help me hear You in Scripture, in a devotion, in a song, or in any way You see fit.

Surprise me this week ahead so I will know that this prayer has been heard.

Thank You, Lord.

Thank You for loving me so and thank You for hearing my prayer.

Thank You for drawing me in deeper still.

I ask all of this in Jesus's Name.

Amen.

Chapter 12

In Our Transparency, the Lord Can Use Us to Help and Bless Others

It was a genuine surprise to wake up at the beginning of December and realize I was about to purchase the last ten gift cards for this assignment the Holy Spirit presented to me. When the Holy Spirit first spoke to me about this proposal, twelve months seemed like a long time. But it went by so fast! I was now at a point where it was second nature to me to have a Chick-fil-A gift card in my purse to hand out when Holy Spirit prompted me, and yet, I had a sense of sadness that this part of my assignment was coming to an end.

Even though I had given away 110 gift cards during the year, the Lord had one more component of this assignment: for the last ten gift cards, I was not to put any Scripture reference on the top of any of them. I was to simply wait until the Holy Spirit gave me the Scripture for the gift card, and then watch as He put the recipient right in front of me that the word was for.

His challenge generated a little anxiety in me, but I was sensing that He was once and for all, going to use this idea to drive out any doubts I might still be having as to whether or not I could hear His Voice clearly. I've talked about the importance of being able to hear His Voice throughout this entire book. Even though I'd been through an eleven-month exercise, there had still been times I had questioned if I was really hearing Him. He wanted to seal the deal and close that door to my doubts once and for all.

The first time this happened, I was driving to Crisis Assistance to drop off some more clothes. Driving through downtown Charlotte, the Holy Spirit interrupted me and He spoke a clear Scripture to me, "Proverbs 16:11." I had no idea what that Scripture was, and immediately pulled out my Bible that I keep in my car to look it up at the next stop light. This is what it says: "Honest scales and balances belong to the LORD; all the weights in the bag are of his making." (Proverbs 16:11)

Then the Lord said, "Put that Scripture on a gift card. This is a word for someone you will see at Crisis Assistance."

Oh boy, I thought. *Here we go.* My intellect and reasoning began to kick in. I started thinking, "I have no idea what that might mean to someone. It makes no sense to me. This is really testing me now." Have you ever had one of those moments when you find yourself running right smack into someone or into a situation you might rather avoid, but you know you have to go on and move forward and acknowledge the person or the event? That's how I felt about whomever I would meet at Crisis Assistance.

At the drop-off center, which was not yet open, I pulled up behind a car that was already in line, parked and waiting. As I was sitting there, that gut reaction I get from the Holy Spirit came. The still, small voice said, "It's for her," and I knew He was talking about the lady in the car ahead of me.

Come on, Lord. Really? These were my thoughts as I was shaking my head. Even though I had no clue how He was going to set it all up, it never dawned on me I would have to get out of my car and approach someone sitting in their car. This person did not know me from Adam.

I grabbed the gift card sitting on the passenger seat. *No way I am going to stop now,* I thought, as this seemed to be a pretty specific appointment. So I opened my car door, got out and walked up to her window. She must have seen me coming through her rearview mirror, because she opened her car door before I got there.

I am not exactly sure what my opening line was . . . I think I first said something like, "I am a believer. Are you?" Hoping of course she would say yes. And when she did, I breathed a sigh of relief. I thought, *Whew! Step one complete.*

I began to tell her the story of how the Lord had me give out gifts cards on occasion to people He put in my path, but this time had been a bit different because He had specifically given me a Scripture to write on this card. I went on to tell her that when I pulled up behind her to wait, He spoke to me and said I was supposed to give it to her.

I'm not sure why I still felt the need to explain things, but I continued by saying I had read the word and never seen it in Scripture before, and had no idea what it meant. (Like I was supposed to? *Good grief*—how could *I* possibly know all Scripture, the meaning of it and what God intended for this woman this day?) I told her that if it wasn't a word for her, she could at least enjoy the gift card. I think then I finally stopped talking.

"Yes ma'am, yes ma'am," she kept saying as she reached out to take the card. "Thank you so much," she said as we exchanged a few more pleasantries. I went back to my car and waited until the drop-off line opened up, all the while hoping and praying that word meant something to her.

When the lane opened, she pulled up and unloaded her car. I sat there almost wishing she would hurry up. I was feeling embarrassed, even a little foolish, wondering if she was thinking she had just had an encounter with a crazy person, and yet I knew I had obeyed. She finally finished unloading all the stuff from the trunk of her car, and as she headed back to get in her driver's seat, she turned around, looked at me, smiled and gave a big wave. I returned a "thumbs up" and off she went.

After I dropped off my clothes and headed back home, I began to process all those feelings of anxiety I'd had. I kept saying to myself, *This is SO not about me!* I thanked the Lord that He was stretching me further still and was happy I had followed through. I found myself praying once again that He would remove anything in me that still had concerns about what others think.

Truthfully, I am so over that life-stealing spirit, worrying about what people think. I see so many people struggling, trying to be "just right," whatever that really even means. The older I get and the more I come into a true sense of knowing who I am, I find it is becoming easier to just be me. It is sad to see so many trying to keep up with the Joneses, so many trying to live by the world's views of excellence, so many trying to keep up appearances, that they or their family is all together, when behind closed doors life is falling apart. I have one young friend who is always saying, "We all have junk!" and it's true. But I don't see too many people owning that. I see a lot of people pretending that everything is perfect.

As a family, we have come into a new season of being real. My son Rob has given me permission to share a little of his story.

Halfway through Rob's junior high school year, he made the

decision to enter a local outpatient rehab program here in Charlotte called The Insight Program. This all went down the month of January, the same month I began Project 120 and the same month my parents decided to move. The Lord's timing is always a mystery. Maybe now you can understand why that laugh I had in Roanoke was some good medicine I really needed.

Rob had some struggles during his high school years, and began smoking pot on a regular basis. Things came to a head, and in January 2014, once he met with Steve, the director of Insight, Rob made the decision to enter the program and get some help. And he has not looked back! It's has been an amazing ride for all of us, a blessing for him and for our family, far beyond anything we could have ever hoped for or imagined. I've prayed for Rob's and Hallie's destiny their entire lives. Let me tell you, I did not have a clue that part of his journey would look like this.

The Lord knows I do not want to be that kind of daughter who pretends to be something or someone I am not. It's not always easy to be authentic and I'm not saying I get it right all the time. I also have learned there are times I should be discerning. Some things are not meant to be shared and should stay personal. There is a Scripture in Matthew 7 that says, "Don't throw your pearls before swine." I have learned that some people are not safe to share my pearls with. But my prayer is that the Holy Spirit will always help

me be truthful and open and real about my life and my walk with
Him.

From the get go, Rob's dad and I both agreed that we wanted
to be open about what was going on in our family. We wanted to
be real and true. So we asked Rob about how to move forward with
this news and he said, "As long as you tell people I am the one who
made the decision, you can tell anyone you want." And so we have.
We have been pretty much an open book to everyone whose path we
have crossed who has asked, "How is Rob?" We made the decision
as a family that we were not going to answer with the typical reply,
"Oh, everything is great!" We wanted to be credible. And I have
to tell you, it has been liberating for us to be open and transparent
instead of trying to look "just right." And what we have found is
when we are authentic and open with others about what is going
on in our lives, the very people we have been real with have opened
up and shared their stuff with us. It's been remarkable, really. In our
transparency, the Lord has been able to use us to help others who are
where we have been.

So whether in gift card giving or being open about personal
family matters, I want to be me in all that and everything in
between. I want to be the daughter the Lord created. I believe that
gives Him honor and I now see it is an important part of our calling.
Doing something for the Lord that He calls us to do is great and it is

part of walking in our destiny, but *being* who God has called us to be is His deepest desire for us as His children. When we can walk in our genuine, legitimate identity, we can truly glorify Him.

Chapter 13

Love with Action

The last month of Project 120 continued to be a whole new adventure of its own.

My son Rob needed some new khakis. That boy can wear out a pair of khakis like nothing I have ever seen. My usual "go-to" store had none in his size, and when I checked online, I found his size was out of stock. So I had to make a trip to the mall to try and find another store that would have what I was looking for.

Sure enough, I easily found a place that sold khakis and had his size in stock. As I was checking out, talking to the cashier about boys' pant sizes, the Holy Spirit whispered "Matthew 21:21" in my ear. The more I chatted with the woman, the more I knew this was someone I needed to give a gift card to. I now knew what Scripture the Lord wanted me to put on it.

While checking out, she began talking to me about other styles of pants they sold, and I began to think I should maybe look at one other style. She too had a slim teen son the same age, so off she went to find the different style she thought I might like. While she was gone, I have to admit, before I wrote the Scripture on top of the gift card, I pulled out my phone and Googled Mathew 21:21. I wanted to make sure there actually was a Mathew 21:21!

No sooner did I see that there actually was a twenty-first verse in Matthew 21, the woman returned. I put my phone away and inconspicuously got a gift card out, writing "Matthew 21:21" at the top of the card. Since I was the only one at the counter, she quickly rang me up for the two pairs of khakis and handed me my bag of pants. The time had come.

I launched into my now well-rehearsed opening, and told her that while I had been waiting for her to get the second pair of pants, the Holy Spirit had spoken "Mathew 21:21" to me to put on a gift card to give to her. I went on to say I had not even known if there was such a Scripture, but had checked and sure enough there was. "Maybe this is a word for you for today or maybe even for the year ahead," I said as I handed her the gift card.

This time there was not the familiar tears and big hug, but she seemed noticeably touched by the gesture and we continued to talk. She said that she would be thinking about how to share this story with her coworkers, that she was going to ponder what it would look like to pay it forward. As this conversation came to a close, we smiled at one another and I said good-bye. I told her I would be checking back in the next time I was at the mall to see what had happened.

You can imagine my complete surprise when, the very next day, at Rob's YMCA intramural basketball game, there on the other side of the bleachers on the opposing team's side, was the woman who had sold me the khakis. The Lord cracks me up!

I tapped my hubby Rob on the shoulder and pointing to her, told him she was the lady I had given a gift card to the day earlier. I decided to wait until halftime to say hello.

Laura got just as much of a kick out of seeing me as I did seeing her. We visited during halftime, and we pointed our sons out to each other. She said she was still thinking about the gift card and asked if we could exchange e-mails, which we did. I told her I thought this setup was surely designed by God, and He seemed to be connecting us. When the buzzer sounded, letting us know halftime was over, we hugged and I went back to my seat on the other side of the bleachers. When we left that day, I hoped I would hear from her, because when I got home, but I could not find her e-mail address anywhere. But I knew where to find her at the mall and truthfully, thought no more about it after that.

Out of the blue, six weeks later, as I was going to bed and getting ready to turn my phone off, I heard a *ding*. I decided to see who might be sending me mail, and lo and behold, it was from Laura. This is what she wrote:

Hi Anne ~

To reintroduce myself, I am Laura, who sold you the khakis, and in that crazy coincidence—also from the YMCA basketball game when our sons were playing each other. You gave me a Chick-fil-A gift card. I still have it actually, and I have been waiting for the right moment to know how I was going to pay that act of kindness forward. I wasn't going to force it—I was just waiting for inspiration.

I am excited to tell you that tonight it hit me! I was doing a little shopping in PetSmart. I am a huge animal lover. I stopped to chat with a young couple in their twenties—well initially, I had stopped to talk to their dog. Anyway, they told me that they had just found this precious puppy in the street today. I didn't ask exactly where, but based on the story, it did not sound like a highly populated area. He was wearing a collar, but he was thin so he must have been on his own for a little while. The young man said he and his brother had stood outside flagging down cars for over an hour to see if anyone knew the dog. They took him to a vet and checked for a microchip and he had none. The vet said the pup was about 9 months old, but he certainly looked younger. Instead of taking the poor pup to animal control where he would have faced a questionable fate, this couple did not hesitate to open their hearts and home to him and were there buying supplies. I could tell this lucky pup was found by just the right couple.

I thanked them for being so awesome and made my own purchases and got in my car and started driving. That is when it hit me—I wanted to pay it forward to that couple. I turned my car around, went back to PetSmart, purchased a gift card and went to look for them, hoping I hadn't missed them. Luckily, I found them right away and I clumsily told them that their kindness toward the pup had moved me so much that I wanted to help them. (Poor kids—I almost cried but they were very polite). I told them that a complete stranger had done something really nice for me and I wanted to pay it forward. They graciously accepted my gift card and were very appreciative.

Anyway I just wanted to follow up with you. :) Thanks for starting the chain of events.

Regards, Laura

Once again, I was being shown the beautiful array of God's creativity on display. I was also being reminded that the Holy Spirit operates in each one of us individually and uniquely. My way of blessing, Laura's way of blessing, and your way of blessing will look different, and that is a good thing! How boring it would be if we all gave in the same way. Laura chose to take action. She made a conscious decision to step out of her comfort zone and give where she saw a need. It reminds me of a Scripture in 1 John that says, "If anyone has material possessions and sees a brother or sister in need but has no pity on them, how can the love of God be in that person? Dear children, let us not love with words or speech but with actions and in truth." (1 John 3:17-18)

I encourage you to step out of your comfort zone today. Choose to display an act of kindness to another by an action, not through words or speech. Invite the Holy Spirit to give you an opportunity to be a blessing and listen for His suggestion. You will hear Him when He gives you a nudge. It is through our actions that we can demonstrate the kind of love Jesus calls us to operate in. And in those actions of love, we are being who it is He created us to be.

Chapter 14

See Yourself as One of His Beloved

One of the Glory Girls, Carol, has a birthday the end of December, so her sister Ann decided to try and get a group of us together for a surprise birthday luncheon. Ten of us ended up at a local restaurant in our own private room with sliding doors that could be shut to allow for privacy. It was a great break from all the Christmas busyness and it was wonderful being with everyone who could attend.

It was not too long after we all greeted one another that we sat down and our conversation turned toward the Lord. Jiljane had just gotten back from a fabulous trip to the Galapagos Islands and we listened as she shared stories of her magnificent adventure exploring some of the islands, describing God's creation all around her. Marcia was looking totally amazing after having just had a partial mastectomy, and we were praising God for His faithfulness to her and His healing power that was evident in these few short weeks after surgery.

Carol then began sharing about fruit she was having with a new inner-healing ministry technique called Splankna that she had become trained and efficient in for her counseling. We were getting caught up in the awe of God as testimony after testimony was being shared.

All the while, our waiter, Brian, continued to come in and out of the room as drinks and food needed to be served. We did not try and quiet our conversation when he came around. We simply kept talking like we would if we were sitting in my den at my home, pondering and processing out loud all we were gleaning from one another. The Spirit of God was ever present, that weighty Presence all of us have come to know and appreciate. Psalm 22:3 reminds us that He inhabits the praises of His people and Matthew 18:20 says when two or three are gathered, He is in the midst. Lunch was eventually served, and we continued to enjoy one another and the Holy Spirit's Presence.

When the time came to pay, we all agreed that Brian had been a great waiter and we wanted to leave him a nice tip. I got my usual gut reaction when I wondered if I should leave him a gift card too, so I told the girls I would be adding that as well. I then felt led to ask them all to pray and ask the Holy Spirit to confirm what Scripture I should put on the top of the card. "Brian needs to know that he is God's beloved son in whom He is well pleased," someone said, and there was an immediate unanimous agreement. I pulled out the gift card and wrote those words on it and I referenced Matthew 3:17, which is the Scripture where God the Father speaks these words over His Son, Jesus.

We pooled our monies for a nice tip and added the gift card to the bill. When Brian came to pick up the bill, we thanked him for all he had done and told him we did not need any change. We began gathering our belongings and Carol was getting her gifts and cards together to leave when Brian showed back up. We all stopped what we were doing and listened as he spoke.

"Thank you all so much for this gracious tip and gift card. I really appreciate it. I want you to know that I am aware that I am a sinner saved by Grace."

I was standing right in front of him when he said this and in an instant, I began to speak. "Brian, I want to suggest that you have a mindset shift, beginning today. I want to encourage you to look at yourself through a different set of lenses. Instead of thinking of yourself as a sinner, how about in 2015 you begin to see yourself as a beloved son of the Father God in whom He is well pleased."

You could feel the unction of the Holy Spirit on those words, and we all saw his reaction as I spoke them. It was like they hit him, that's the best way I know how to describe it. He heard those words and received them instantly. Something supernatural happened: his eyes changed. They lit up and he began to smile. We all watched as he nodded his head in agreement and said he would. It was a beautiful ending to a Holy moment, and a wonderful time together.

Psalm 139 is one Scripture that tells us about how special we are to the Lord. I love reading this Psalm in different translations. Carol gave me a book, *The Passion Translation of The Psalms—Poetry on Fire*, for my birthday, and when you read Psalm 139 from this translation, you can't help but see yourself the way the Lord does. I've included several of the verses at the end of the chapter. Imagine the Father Himself reading the words to you.

Later that day, Ellen, one of Carol's daughters who had had lunch with us, called to tell her mom she could feel waves of the Holy Spirit flowing over her during the entire time we were together. I love that the Lord blessed Ellen, too, that day as she sat and listened to us all share and talk about the Lord.

Carol was honored for her birthday and The Lord was honored as well as we made Him the center of Carol's birthday celebration. And Carol's birthday celebration, which turned into an impromptu prayer meeting, blessed Brian as well, as he was given a word of life all through the simple gesture of a gift card.

Verses from Psalm 139 — The Passion Translation:

Lord, you know everything there is to know about me.

You've examined my innermost being
with your loving gaze. (1)

You are so intimately aware of me, Lord, You read my heart
like an open book and you know all the words
I'm about to speak before I even start a sentence! (3)

With your hand of love upon my life, you
impart a Father's blessing to me.

This is just too wonderful, deep
and incomprehensible!

Your understanding of me brings wonder
and strength. (5b-6)

I thank you, God, for making me
so mysteriously complex!

Everything you do is marvelously breathtaking.

It simply amazes me to think about it!

How thoroughly you know me, Lord! (14)

You even formed every bone in my body when you
created me in the secret place; carefully,
skillfully shaping me from nothing to something. (15)

You saw who you created me to be,
before I became me!

Before I'd ever seen the light of day,
the number of days you planned for me
were already written in your book.

Every single moment you are thinking of me!

How precious and wonderful to consider,
that you cherish me constantly in your every thought.

O God, your desires toward me are more than the grains of sand
on every shore! (16-18)

Chapter 15

Simple Kindness Can Make
a Huge Difference

God is a God of order. Even though the Holy Spirit is described as being "like the wind," (Acts 2:2) one can see throughout the entire Bible that Father God creates and orchestrates things in His perfect ways and timing. So now that I think more about it, I guess it should have come as no surprise to me that the Lord asked me to give the last gift card, #120, to Lisa, the woman I had given the first card to at the grocery store. The first phase of this wonderful assignment was coming to a close, and I was hopeful Lisa would be blessed to see me again.

I headed back to the Harris Teeter at the end of December to find Lisa. It took three visits until I was finally able to connect with her. By the time I did, the New Year had begun.

It was eleven in the morning when I arrived and I saw her back behind the deli counter. I called out her name and asked her if she recognized me. She nodded that she did and smiled at me. I asked her if she had a few minutes to spare, that I wanted to share something with her. She came out from behind the counter and gave me a hug. I told her I was glad to see her and that I had an ending to the story that began a year ago.

I retold the story of how the gift card giving had begun, reminding her that she was the first person I had given one to.

"Oh, I still have it," she said.

"What?" I asked.

"I still have it," she said again, and she pulled out a wallet from her pocket and began going through it. There, tucked in between all kinds of cards and coupons, she pulled out a worn-looking Chick-fil-A gift card. "I'm still waiting to give it away. I told my pastor about you and what had happened and I know when the time is right, I will give it to the right person."

I couldn't believe it. I never thought someone would hold on to one of the gift cards! And hers did not even have a Scripture on it. All it had written on it was the Name "Jesus" and the money amount of ten dollars.

"Well here's the deal," I continued. "I have one card left. I have given away one hundred nineteen gift cards and the Lord specifically said I was to bring the 120th card here and give it to you. I also have started putting Scripture references on the cards and the Holy Spirit said Psalm 23 was the Scripture I was supposed to put on it." I pulled the card out of my pocket and gave it to her. "Psalm 23 is the Psalm for the year. It is a word for you for this year ahead." At this point, yes, you guessed it, she was crying and hugging me and thanking me and once again seemed overwhelmed.

I told her it might be time to use that first card or give it away now that she had a new one. I am not sure whether or not she heeded my advice. I told her that I was planning on writing a book to tell about the year of gift card giving and that she would be in it.

"I want to buy a copy," she said.

"Don't you worry," I responded, "I will be happy to give one to you."

As I was leaving, she went back behind the counter and I could see her telling her coworkers what had just happened. I had a sense they knew about the first gift card Lisa had received as she pointed her finger my way, and her fellow employees looked and smiled.

Lisa's hands and feet became Jesus's Hands and Feet as she shared the story. Once again, the Kingdom of God was being released, behind a deli counter no less. And once again, I saw how the simplest kindness can make a difference, shining a light brightly for His Name's sake. Giving Lisa the first card had been a bit more complicated, but this straightforward ending was just as lovely and rewarding. The most elementary way of giving can minister to a heart and open a blessing. All we have to do is listen to His Voice and follow Him.

Conclusion

When I sit and ponder all that took place that year, I find myself in a mode of constant thanksgiving. I can see tangibly how God Himself took over many events in my life and the life of my family to get us to where we are today. In the midst of a lot of ups and downs, transitions and new beginnings, there is today an evident peace, joy, contentment, and love in my home and in my family.

While wrapping up Project 120, the Holy Spirit dropped Deuteronomy 11:11 into my spirit. I immediately went to my Bible to refresh my memory as to exactly what Deuteronomy 11:11 says. I knew it had something to do with crossing over the Jordan river into the promised land—it's a Scripture I have looked at more times than I can count—but I did not know it verbatim and wanted to see exactly what the message was.

Once I opened it and read it, I knew it was a word for me.

But the land you are crossing the Jordan to take possession of is a land of mountains and valleys that drinks rain from heaven. It is a land the Lord your God cares for; the eyes of the Lord your God are continually on it from the beginning of the year to its end. So if you faithfully obey the commands I am giving you today—to love the Lord your God and to serve him with all your heart and with all your soul—then I will send rain on your land in its season, both autumn and spring rains, so that you may gather in your grain, new wine and olive oil. I will provide grass in the fields for your cattle, and you will eat and be satisfied.

Deuteronomy 11:11-15

The eyes of the Lord have been on this project from the beginning of the year to the end and as He has sent the rain, His Presence, to my land, this endeavor. I expect to see His Provision come forth in beautiful, fascinating, and curious ways as I continue to listen for His Voice and follow Him. His promises are sure.

Recently, I had a vision and a dream. I saw both as signs of where I had been and where I was going.

In the vision (a vision happens when your eyes are closed but you are awake), I was in a green graduation cap and gown in my bedroom. Green is a color for new life, new beginnings, and rest. In the vision, I watched myself as I threw my cap up into the air, signaling a graduation had occurred.

In the dream I had, I was at Glory of Zion at an orientation event on a large campus. I was directed to building number 5 (5 is the number for Grace) to attend my last orientation event for the day. When I entered the building, there were lots of people waiting in the foyer. I saw a narrow staircase heading to a room upstairs. When the crowd began to move toward the stairwell, I was supernaturally pushed to the front of the crowd and I found myself on the narrow staircase heading up the steps to the upper room. When I got to the top of the steps, I saw the room was close to being full, but there were enough seats left so that I would be able to sit in one. The professor came out to make an announcement, and I woke up.

The stairwell is a symbol of transition, taking steps toward something. Heading to the upper room is a sign of moving higher in the things of the Holy Spirit. Knowing there was a seat for me let me know it was time for me to be there. I had completed a season and had graduated, and now was being moved and positioned for a new time of learning and growing in the Spirit. As one aspect of Project 120 is now complete, it is time for the next phase to begin.

Cultivating intimacy with the Holy Spirit by pressing in to hear

His Voice and then choosing to follow Him continues to challenge, excite, surprise, and motivate me. Having a relationship with the Holy Spirit has helped me know myself better and has helped me deepen my relationship with God the Father and with Jesus.

Invite the Holy Spirit in to your life today. Ask Him to speak to you in new ways. Open your eyes and pay attention to those around you. Lend your ear to His Voice and His prompting. He is speaking. And you can hear Him. You are one of His sheep and He needs you in this world today. He is ready to share more of Himself with you and use you to be one of His ambassadors if you are willing, and when you are willing, He will take you places and introduce you to people you can't dream of.

I hope that you, too, feel more challenged, excited, surprised, and motivated seeing that something as simple as giving out a gift card at the Lord's leading can take you on a magnificent journey with Him. I wonder what idea He will plant in your heart to share His goodness and loving kindness with another. This is what I do know: there is no greater joy than when we chose to listen to His Voice and follow Him.

Blessings,

Anne

For I fully expect and hope that I will never be ashamed, but that I will continue to be bold for Christ, as I have been in the past. And I trust that my life will bring honor to Christ, whether I live or die.

Philippians 1:20

Journal Pages

Journal Pages

Journal Pages